Bundt

Cake

Recipes

30 Delicious Bundt Cake Recipes from Scratch

By Marie Folher

Disclaimer

Please note the information contained within this document is for educational and entertainment purposes only. Any of the information shouldn't be taken as medical advice. All effort has been executed to present accurate, up to date, and reliable, complete information. No warranties of any kind are declared or implied. Readers acknowledge that the author is not engaging in the rendering of legal, financial, medical or professional advice. The content within this book has been derived from various sources. Please consult a licensed professional before attempting any techniques outlined in this book.

By reading this document, the reader agrees that under no circumstances is the author responsible for any losses, direct or indirect, which are incurred as a result of the use of the information contained within this document, including, but not limited to, — errors, omissions, or inaccuracies.

Table of Contents

Introduction

There is no denying that one of the favorite cake pans of baker is the humble Bundt pan. From regular chocolate pound cake to an apple cake, it's better to prepare them in a Bundt. Rich and moist Bundt cake is an ultimate dessert that has the power to send your taste buds to gastronomical heaven in just one bite. These old-fashioned Southern cakes have never gone out of style. In fact, they are baker's secret weapon to bring together incredible flavors and presented as a pretty molded cake. Its ring-shaped pan can transform any regular cake into something sensational. And the best part, this culinary art doesn't require any fuss in the kitchen.

Most of the Bundt cakes need simple ingredients, powdered sugar dusting, or a simple glaze to shine. You can bake Bundt cake of just any type to satisfy your particular sweet cravings. These beautiful cakes are perfect for any occasion and meal, from breakfast to dessert, or from holiday get-together to a party, or simply when you are craving for something rich or sweet. However, Bundt cakes are not simple to make, even for a baker who holds intermediate level culinary skills. This shouldn't stop you as any cake recipe can be converted into Bundt cake. You just need a little practice and obviously, faith in yourself.

So what are you waiting for? There's no better time to get started with Bundt cake baking. I have combined some tastiest Bundt cake recipes to begin your baking journey with a Bundt. Choose from a range of flavors from these fantastic ring-shaped sweet treats and get baking. These decadent always bound to wow everyone. Enjoy!

Marbled Bundt Cake with Almond and Chocolate

Preparation time: 15 minutes

Cooking time: 50 minutes

Total time: 65 minutes

Servings: 12

Nutritional Info (Per Serving):

336 kCal | 19 g Fat | 4.9 g Protein | 36 g Carbs | 2 g Fiber | 24 g Sugar

Ingredients:

1 ½ cups / 180-grams white all-purpose flour, sifted, leveled

2 teaspoons baking powder

¾ cup / 75-grams ground almond

1 ¼ cups / 225-grams caster sugar

⅔ cup / 70-grams dark chocolate chip

¾ teaspoon almond extract, unsweetened

¾ cup / 180-grams unsalted butter, softened, and more for greasing

3 large eggs, at room temperature

3 tablespoons cocoa powder

3 tablespoons hot water

2 tablespoons milk

¼ cup / 30-grams icing sugar

Directions:

1.   Switch on the oven, and preheat it to 350 °F / 180 °C.

2.   Meanwhile, take a small bowl, add cocoa powder, pour in hot water, stir well until combined and then set aside until required.

3.   Take a large bowl, place butter in it, add sugar, beat with an electric beater until light and fluffy mixture comes together, and then beat in almond extract until combined.

4.   Add flour in it, along with almonds and baking powder, stir until well combined, then use an electric beater to mix in eggs until incorporated, one egg at a time, and stir in milk until mixed.

5.   Transfer half of the batter in a separate bowl, add prepared cocoa mixture, and stir until well mixed.

6.   Add chocolate chips into the other half of the cake batter and then stir until mixed.

7.   Take a 6 cup / 1.5-liter Bundt pan, grease it with melted butter, dust it with flour, and then use a spoon to pour in prepared batters in alternate layers.

8.   Drag the handle of a spoon to create a marble effect in the batter layers and bake for 40 to 50 minutes until thoroughly cooked and pass the skewer test that comes out clean from the deepest part of the cake.

9.   When cake has baked, let it cool in the pan for 10 minutes, then take it out by turning the pan on a wire rack and cool it for 30 minutes.

10. Once the cake has cooled, dust icing sugar on it, cut it into twelve slices and serve.

Banana and Chocolate Bundt Cake

Preparation time: 20 minutes

Cooking time: 60 minutes

Total time: 80 minutes

Servings: 12

Nutritional Info (Per Serving):

514 kCal | 24.2 g Fat | 9.8 g Protein | 66 g Carbs | 4 g Fiber | 42 g Sugar

Ingredients:

For the Cake:

3 large bananas, peeled

2 ¾ cups / 350-grams self-raising flour, sifted, leveled

1 teaspoon baking soda

3 tablespoons cocoa powder

½ teaspoon salt

1 ¾ cups / 350-grams brown sugar, packed

½ cup / 100-grams dark chocolate chips

¾ cup / 50-grams salted peanuts, chopped

1 teaspoon vanilla extract, unsweetened

3 large eggs, at room temperature

½ cup / 150-grams yogurt

¾ cup / 200-grams unsalted butter, melted, and more for greasing

3 tablespoons hot water

0.6 cup / 150 ml milk, full-fat

For the Glaze:

1 ¼ cups / 80-grams salted peanuts, chopped

¼ cup / 100-grams Dulce de leche caramel

1 tablespoon milk

Directions:

1.   Switch on the oven, and preheat it to 350 °F / 180 °C.

2.   Meanwhile, take a small bowl, add cocoa powder, pour in hot water, stir well until combined and then set aside until required.

3.   Cut the banana into bite-size pieces, add them in a bowl, mash with a form and then whisk in melted butter, vanilla, eggs, and milk until well combined.

4.   Take a separate large bowl, add flour in it along with salt, brown sugar, and baking soda, stir well until mixed, and then gradually stir in the banana mixture until combined.

5.   Transfer half of the batter in a separate bowl, add prepared cocoa mixture, chocolate chips, and 50-grams of yogurt and stir until well mixed.

6.   Add nuts and remaining yogurt into the other half of the cake batter and then stir until mixed.

7.   Take a 10 cup /2.5-liter Bundt pan, grease it with melted butter, dust it with flour, and then use a spoon to pour in prepared batters in alternate layers.

8.   Drag the handle of a spoon to create a marble effect in the batter layers and bake for 1 hour until thoroughly cooked and pass the skewer test that comes out clean from the deepest part of the cake.

9.   Meanwhile, prepare the glaze and for this, place caramel in a small bowl, add milk and stir until well mixed, set aside until required.

10.   When cake has baked, let it cool in the pan for 10 minutes, then take it out by turning the pan on a wire rack and cool it for 30 minutes.

11.   Once the cake has cooled, drizzle prepared glaze on it, sprinkle with peanuts, cut it into twelve slices and then serve.

Blood Orange and Olive Oil Bundt Cake

Preparation time: 15 minutes

Cooking time: 40 minutes

Total time: 55 minutes

Servings: 14

Nutritional Info (Per Serving):

326 kCal | 15.3 g Fat | 4.6 g Protein | 40 g Carbs | 1 g Fiber | 27.3 g Sugar

Ingredients:

For the Cake:

2 ¼ cups / 280g self-raising flour, sifted, leveled

3 blood oranges, zested and juiced, about 0.6 cups/ 150ml juice

1 ½ cups / 300-grams caster sugar

0.6 cup / 150 ml olive oil

5 large eggs, at room temperature

For the Glaze:

0.9 cup / 144-grams white chocolate, chopped

1 blood orange, zested

1 ½ of blood orange, juiced, about 0.3 cup / 75 ml juice

Directions:

1.   Switch on the oven, and preheat it to 350 °F / 180 °C.

2.   Meanwhile, take a large bowl, crack eggs in it, add sugar and orange zest and whisk for 10 minutes until thick mixture comes together.

3.   Whisk on oil and orange juice at medium-low speed until thoroughly combined and then gradually whisk in flour until incorporated.

4.   Take a 10 cup / 2.5-liter Bundt pan, grease it with cooking spray, then add prepared cake batter in it and bake for 35 to 40 minutes until thoroughly cooked and pass the skewer test that comes out clean from the deepest part of the cake.

5.   When cake has baked, let it cool in the pan for 10 minutes, then take it out by turning the pan on a wire rack and cool it for 30 minutes.

6.   Meanwhile, prepare the glaze and for this, take a heatproof bowl, place chocolate in it, microwave for 1 minute or until it has melted, then whisk in orange juice until combined and set aside until required.

7.   Once the cake has cooled, drizzle the glaze on it, sprinkle with orange zest, cut it into fourteen slices and then serve.

Banana Date Cake

Preparation time: 20 minutes

Cooking time: 50 minutes

Total time: 70 minutes

Servings: 8

Nutritional Info (Per Serving):

502 kCal | 30.5 g Fat | 7.3 g Protein | 51 g Carbs | 3.3 g Fiber | 35 g Sugar

Ingredients:

For the Cake:

0.6 cup / 100-grams date, stoned, chopped

2 bananas, diced

1 ½ cups / 200-grams self-raising flour, sifted, leveled

¾ cup / 175-grams unsalted butter, softened, and more for greasing

½ cup / 100-grams muscovado sugar, packed

3 tablespoons honey

1 teaspoon cinnamon

¾ cup / 50-grams chopped walnut

2 large eggs, at room temperature, beaten

For the Glaze:

¾ cup / 50-grams walnuts, halved

0.1 cup / 25-grams unsalted butter

2 tablespoons honey

Directions:

1. Switch on the oven, and preheat it to 320 °F / 160 °C.

2. Meanwhile, take a large bowl, add flour, cinnamon, and sugar in it, stir well and then beat in eggs, butter, and honey until combined and fluffy.

3. Place banana pieces in a small bowl, mash with a fork, then add into prepared batter along with dates and walnuts, and fold until mixed.

4. Take a 6 cup /1.5-liter Bundt pan, grease it with butter, pour in the prepared batter and bake for 40 to 50 minutes until thoroughly cooked and pass the skewer test that comes out clean from the deepest part of the cake.

5. When cake has baked, let it cool in the pan for 15 minutes, then take it out by turning the pan on a wire rack and cool it for 30 minutes.

6. Meanwhile, prepare the glaze and for this, take a small saucepan, place it over medium heat, add butter and honey, stir and cook until butter melts, stirring continuously.

7. Boil the butter mixture for 1 minute or until slightly thickened, then remove the saucepan from heat, add walnuts, stir well, and set aside until cooled and until required.

8. Once the cake has cooled, drizzle glaze on it, cut it into eight slices and then serve.

Soured Cream Bundt Cake

Preparation time: 15 minutes

Cooking time: 40 minutes

Total time: 55 minutes

Servings: 16

Nutritional Info (Per Serving):

209 kCal | 10.9 g Fat | 2 g Protein | 25 g Carbs | 0.7 g Fiber |
18.6 g Sugar

Ingredients:

For the Cake:

1 ½ cups / 180-grams white all-purpose flour, sifted, leveled

1/8 teaspoon salt

1 teaspoon baking powder

1 cup / 180-grams caster sugar

1 teaspoon vanilla extract, unsweetened

½ cup / 125-grams unsalted butter, softened, and more for greasing

2 large eggs, at room temperature, beaten

0.6 cup / 150-grams soured cream

For the Glaze:

½ cup / 100-grams caster sugar

¼ teaspoon vanilla extract, unsweetened

¼ cup / 50-grams unsalted butter

4 tablespoons water

Directions:

1.   Switch on the oven, and preheat it to 350 °F / 180 °C.

2.   Meanwhile, take a medium bowl, add butter and caster sugar in it, and use an electric beater to beat well until combined and fluffy.

3.   Then beat in eggs, one at a time, until blended and then beat in vanilla extract.

4.   Take another medium bowl, add flour in it, stir in salt and baking powder until mixed, and then gradually mix half of this mixture into the butter mixture, 3 tablespoons at a time, until incorporated.

5.   Beat in half of the sour cream until well combined, then beat in remaining flour mixture and sour cream until well mixed.

6.   Take a 6 cup / 1.5-liter Bundt pan, grease it with melted butter, dust it with flour, then add prepared cake batter in it and bake for 40 minutes until thoroughly cooked and pass the skewer test that comes out clean from the deepest part of the cake.

7.   When cake has baked, let it cool in the pan for 5 minutes, then take it out by turning the pan on a wire rack and cool it for 30 minutes.

8.   Meanwhile, prepare the glaze and for this, take a small saucepan, place it over medium heat, add all the ingredients in it and cook for 5 minutes until the butter has melted.

9.   Bring the glaze to boil, then reduce heat to lower level, simmer the glaze for 3 minutes, then set aside to cool and until required.

10.   Once the cake has cooled, drizzle glaze on it, cut it into sixteen slices and then serve.

Chocolate Peppermint Bundt Cake

Preparation time: 15 minutes

Cooking time: 45 minutes

Total time: 60 minutes

Servings: 12

Nutritional Info (Per Serving):

322 kCal | 18.4 g Fat | 4.6 g Protein | 35 g Carbs | 2 g Fiber | 25 g Sugar

Ingredients:

For the Cake:

2 cups / 250-grams white all-purpose flour, sifted, leveled, and more for dusting

⅓ cup / 50-grams cocoa powder

1 ¾ cups / 350-grams granulated white sugar, packed

1 teaspoon salt

1 ½ teaspoons baking soda

1 cup / 225-grams unsalted butter, and more for greasing

1 teaspoon vanilla extract, unsweetened

1 ½ teaspoons peppermint extract, unsweetened

½ cup / 120-grams sour cream

2 large eggs, at room temperature

1 cup / 240 ml water

½ cup peppermint candies

For the Glaze:

1 ½ tablespoon corn syrup

1 ½ tablespoon granulated white sugar

0.7 cup / 112-grams chocolate, bittersweet, chopped

½ cup / 120-grams heavy cream

Directions:

1. Switch on the oven, and preheat it to 350 °F / 175 °C.

2. Meanwhile, take a small saucepan, place it over medium heat, add cocoa powder, salt, and butter, pour in water, and cook for 5 minutes until the butter has melted and combined, whisking continuously, set aside until required.

3. Take a large bowl, add flour in it and then stir in baking soda and sugar until mixed.

4. Whisk in half of the cocoa mixture until blended and then whisk in the remaining cocoa mixture until well combined and thick mixture comes together.

5. Add peppermint and vanilla extract, and sour cream and whisk until smooth.

6. Take a 12 cup /3-liter Bundt pan, add prepared cake batter in it and bake for 40 to 45 minutes until thoroughly cooked and pass the skewer test that comes out clean from the deepest part of the cake.

7. Meanwhile, prepare the glaze and for this, take a medium bowl, add chocolate chips and corn syrup, stir until just mixed and set aside until required.

8. Take a small saucepan, place it over medium heat, add cream stir in sugar and cook for 5 minutes until the cream is hot and sugar has dissolved.

9.   Pour the hot cream mixture over chocolate chips mixture, continue whisking until the chocolate has melted and set aside until required.

10. When cake has baked, let it cool in the pan for 10 minutes, then take it out by turning the pan on a wire rack and cool it for 30 minutes.

11.   Once the cake has cooled, drizzle glaze on it, cut it into twelve slices and then serve.

Monkey Bread

Preparation time: 180 minutes

Cooking time: 45 minutes

Total time: 225 minutes

Servings: 12

Nutritional Info (Per Serving):

533 kCal | 26.1 g Fat | 8 g Protein | 63.7 g Carbs | 2.1 g Fiber | 33 g Sugar

Ingredients:

For the Cake:

5 cups / 625-grams white all-purpose flour, sifted, leveled

¼ cup / 50-grams granulated white sugar, packed

1 teaspoon salt

2 ¼ teaspoons yeast

⅓ cup / 75-grams unsalted butter, melted, and more for greasing

2 large eggs, at room temperature

1 ½ cups / 350 ml milk, warmed

For the Coating:

⅔ cup / 130-grams brown sugar, packed

1 ¼ cups / 250-grams granulated white sugar, packed

1 teaspoon vanilla extract, unsweetened

1 tablespoon cinnamon

¾ cup / 175-grams unsalted butter, divided

For the Vanilla Icing:

1 cup / 120-grams confectioners' sugar

½ teaspoon vanilla extract, unsweetened

3 tablespoons milk, unsweetened

Directions:

1.   Prepare the dough and for this, add yeast in the bowl of a stand mixer, stir in sugar and yeast until well mixed, then cover it and let it stand for 5 minutes.

2.   After 5 minutes, beat in 1 cup /125g flour, salt, butter, and eggs on low speed until combined and then beat in remaining flour until incorporated and the dough comes together, scraping the sides of the bowl.

3.   Keep beating the dough for another 2 minutes, then transfer it into a bowl greased with oil, cover with an aluminum foil and let it rest for 2 hours at a warm place until double in size.

4.   Meanwhile, prepare the coating and for this, take a medium heatproof bowl, add ½ cup / 115g butter and microwave for 2 minutes until it has melted, set aside until required.

5.   Take another medium bowl, add cinnamon and sugar, stir until mixed and set aside until required.

6.   Prepare the Bundt pan, and for this, take a 12 cup / 3 liter Bundt pan, grease it with butter, and set aside until required.

7.   When the dough has risen, transfer it to a working space, punch it down and divide the dough into 40 to 45 balls, about 1.2-inch / 3-cm in diameter.

8.   Dip the balls into melted butter, coat them with cinnamon mixture and then arrange them in the prepared Bundt pan.

9.   Cover the pan with plastic wrap and then let it rest for 20 minutes at a warm place.

10. Meanwhile, switch on the oven, set it to 350 °F / 175 °C and let it preheat.

11. Place the remaining ¼ cup / 60g butter from the coating ingredients in a medium heatproof bowl, then microwave for 2 minutes until it melts, and whisk in vanilla and brown sugar until well mixed.

12. Pour this butter mixture over prepared monkey bread and bake for 45 minutes until golden brown, thoroughly cooked, and pass the skewer test that comes out clean from the deepest part of the cake.

13. When cake has baked, let it cool in the pan for 10 minutes, then take it out by turning the pan on a wire rack and cool it for 30 minutes.

14. Meanwhile, prepare the icing and for this, place all its ingredients in a medium bowl, whisk until combined, and set aside until required.

15. Once the cake has cooled, dust icing sugar on it, cut it into twelve slices and then serve.

Grapefruit and Poppy Seed Cake

Preparation time: 15 minutes

Cooking time: 50 minutes

Total time: 65 minutes

Servings: 8

Nutritional Info (Per Serving):

607 kCal | 30.2 g Fat | 7.5 g Protein | 80.4 g Carbs | 2.5 g Fiber | 55 g Sugar

Ingredients:

For the Cake:

2 grapefruits, zested

2 ½ cups / 300-grams white all-purpose flour sifted, leveled

1½ teaspoon baking powder

1 ½ cups / 300-grams caster sugar

4 teaspoons poppy seed, toasted

1 teaspoon vanilla extract, unsweetened

¾ cup / 175-grams unsalted butter, softened, and more for greasing

1 cup / 225 ml soured cream

3 large eggs, at room temperature

3 tablespoons grapefruit juice

For the Icing:

1 grapefruit, zested

½ cup / 100-grams caster sugar

0.1 cup / 25-grams unsalted butter

4 tablespoons grapefruit juice

Directions:

1.   Switch on the oven, then set it to 350 °F / 180 °C, and let it preheat.

2.   Meanwhile, take a medium bowl, add butter in it and beat in sugar until fluffy.

3.   Then beat in eggs, one at a time, flour, 3 tablespoons at a time, grapefruit zest and juice, baking powder, sour cream, and poppy seeds until incorporated.

4.   Take a 6 cup / 1.5-liter Bundt pan, grease it with butter, then add prepared cake batter in it and bake for 40 to 50 minutes until thoroughly cooked and pass the skewer test that comes out clean from the deepest part of the cake.

5.   When cake has baked, let it cool in the pan for 10 minutes, then take it out by turning the pan on a wire rack and cool it for 30 minutes.

6.   Meanwhile, prepare the icing and for this, place a small saucepan over medium heat, pour in grapefruit juice, sugar, and butter, stir and bring the mixture to boil.

7.   Then switch heat to medium-low level, simmer icing for 3 minutes, and remove the saucepan from heat.

8.   Stir grapefruit zest in the icing and let it cool until required.

9.   Once the cake has cooled, drizzle icing on it, cut it into eight slices, and then serve.

Lemon Poppy Seed Bundt Cake

Preparation time: 15 minutes

Cooking time: 50 minutes

Total time: 65 minutes

Servings: 10

Nutritional Info (Per Serving):

498 kCal | 33.7 g Fat | 10.1 g Protein | 50.6 g Carbs | 1.2 g Fiber | 24 g Sugar

Ingredients:

For the Cake:

2 ¾ cup / 345-grams white all-purpose flour, sifted, leveled

¾ cup / 170-grams unsalted butter, softened, and more for greasing

1 teaspoon salt

1 teaspoon baking powder

2 cups /400-grams granulated white sugar, packed

3 tablespoons poppy seeds

2 tablespoons lemon zest

½ teaspoon baking soda

1/3 cup / 80 ml lemon juice

2 teaspoons vanilla extract, unsweetened

¼ cup / 60 ml olive oil

1 cup / 235-grams sour cream

4 large eggs, at room temperature

For the Glaze:

1 cup/ 120-grams confectioner's sugar

3 tablespoons lemon juice

Directions:

1.   Switch on the oven, then set it to 350 °F / 175 °C, and let it preheat.

2.   Meanwhile, take a medium bowl, add flour in it and then stir in salt, baking powder and soda, and poppy seeds and set aside until required.

3.   Take another medium bowl, add butter in it, beat in sugar until fluffy and then beat in eggs, one at a time and vanilla until combined.

4.   Whisk in flour mixture, 3 tablespoons at a time, until well mixed and then whisk in sour cream until incorporated.

5.   Take a 12 cup / 3-liter Bundt pan, grease it with melted butter, dust it with flour, then add prepared cake batter in it, bake for 45 - 50 minutes until thoroughly cooked, and pass the skewer test that comes out clean from the deepest part of the cake.

6.   When cake has baked, let it cool in the pan for 10 minutes, then take it out by turning the pan on a wire rack and cool it for 30 minutes.

7.   Meanwhile, prepare the glaze and for this, take a small bowl, add lemon juice in it and stir in sugar until thoroughly combined, set aside until required.

8.   Once the cake has cooled, drizzle glaze on it, cut it into ten slices, and then serve.

Blood Orange Cake

Preparation time: 15 minutes

Cooking time: 60 minutes

Total time: 75 minutes

Servings: 12

Nutritional Info (Per Serving):

376 kCal | 19 g Fat | 7.3 g Protein | 39.4 g Carbs | 0.8 g Fiber | 32.1 g Sugar

Ingredients:

For the Cake:

3 cups / 375-grams white all-purpose flour, sifted, leveled

1 ¼ teaspoons salt

1 ½ teaspoons baking powder

2 ½ cups / 500-grams granulated white sugar, packed

½ teaspoon baking soda

2 ½ tablespoons blood orange zest

1 ⅓ cup / 310-grams unsalted butter, softened, and more for greasing

2 ½ teaspoons orange liquor

1 ½ teaspoons vanilla extract, unsweetened

5 large eggs, at room temperature

1 cup / 240 ml blood orange juice

For the Glaze:

1 cup / 120-grams powdered sugar

½ teaspoon vanilla extract, unsweetened

3 tablespoons blood orange juice

Directions:

1. Switch on the oven, then set it to 350 °F / 175 °C, and let it preheat.

2. Meanwhile, take a medium bowl, add orange juice and zest, vanilla, orange liqueur, and eggs and whisk until blended.

3. Place another large bowl, add flour in it, add baking soda, salt, sugar, baking powder, and stir until combined.

4. Then beat in butter, one tablespoon at a time, until mixture resembles crumbs, and then whisk the egg mixture until smooth and fluffy mixture comes together.

5. Take a 15 cup / 3.75-liter Bundt pan, grease it with melted butter, dust it with flour, then add prepared cake batter in it and bake for 1 hour until thoroughly cooked and pass the skewer test that comes out clean from the deepest part of the cake.

6. When cake has baked, let it cool in the pan for 20 minutes, then take it out by turning the pan on a wire rack and cool it for 30 minutes.

7. Meanwhile, prepare the glaze and for this, place all its ingredients in a small bowl and stir until well combined.

8. Once the cake has cooled, drizzle glaze on it, cut it into twelve slices and then serve.

Butter Bundt Cake

Preparation time: 15 minutes

Cooking time: 55 minutes

Total time: 70 minutes

Servings: 12

Nutritional Info (Per Serving):

408 kCal | 19.7 g Fat | 5 g Protein | 56.2 g Carbs | 1.8 g Fiber | 22.9g Sugar

Ingredients:

For the Cake:

3 cups / 375-grams white all-purpose flour, sifted, leveled

1 teaspoon baking powder

2 cups / 400-grams granulated white sugar, packed

1 teaspoon salt

½ teaspoon baking soda

2 teaspoons vanilla extract, unsweetened

1 cup / 230-grams unsalted butter, softened, and more for greasing

1 cup / 240 ml buttermilk

4 large eggs, at room temperature

For the Sauce:

¾ cup / 150-grams granulated white sugar, packed

1/3 cup / 75-grams unsalted butter, softened

3 tablespoons water

2 teaspoons vanilla extract, unsweetened

Directions:

1. Switch on the oven, set it to 325 °F / 165 °C and let it preheat.

2. Meanwhile, take a large bowl, place flour in it, add remaining ingredients for the cake in it and beat until incorporated and smooth batter comes together.

3. Take a 12 cup / 3 liter Bundt pan, grease it with melted butter, dust it with flour, then add prepared cake batter in it and bake for 55 minutes until thoroughly cooked and pass the skewer test that comes out clean from the deepest part of the cake.

4. Meanwhile, prepare the sauce and for this, take a small saucepan, place it over low heat, add butter, sugar, vanilla, and water, and cook for 3 minutes until the butter has melted, stirring continuously, set aside until required.

5. When cake has baked, pour prepared sauce on it, let it cool in the pan for 10 minutes or until the sauce has absorbed, then take it out by turning the pan on a plate and cool it for 30 minutes.

6. Once the cake has cooled, cut it into twelve slices, and then serve.

Lemon Lavender Cake

Preparation time: 15 minutes

Cooking time: 50 minutes

Total time: 65 minutes

Servings: 8

Nutritional Info (Per Serving):

305 kCal | 13 g Fat | 4 g Protein | 44.1 g Carbs | 7.5 g Fiber | 24.7g Sugar

Ingredients:

For the Cake:

1½ cups / 188-grams white all-purpose flour, sifted, leveled

¼ teaspoon baking soda

¼ teaspoon salt

1 cup / 200-grams granulated white sugar, packed

1¼ teaspoon dried lavender

1 lemon, zested

1 teaspoon vanilla extract, unsweetened

2 tablespoons lemon juice

½ cup / 110-grams unsalted butter, softened, and more for greasing

2 large eggs, at room temperature

½ cup / 120 ml buttermilk

1¼ teaspoon dried lavender buds

For the Glaze:

1 tablespoon lemon juice

2 teaspoons buttermilk

1 cup / 120-grams powdered sugar

Directions:

1. Switch on the oven, set it to 325 °F / 165 °C, and let it preheat.

2. Meanwhile, take a small bowl, add sugar and lemon zest in it and mash with a spoon until the mixture becomes wet.

3. Take a large bowl, add butter in it, beat in lemon zest mixture for 3 minutes until fluffy, and then beat in eggs, one at a time, until incorporated.

4. Take a medium bowl, place flour in it, and stir in salt and baking soda until mixed.

5. Crush the lavender buds, add them into flour mixture along with dried lavender and stir until combined.

6. Take a measuring cup, add lemon juice, vanilla, and buttermilk, whisk until combined, and then gradually whisk this mixture into flour mixture until incorporated and smooth batter comes together.

7. Take a 6 cup /1.5-liter Bundt pan, grease it with melted butter, dust it with flour, then add prepared cake batter in it and bake for 40 to 50 minutes until thoroughly cooked and pass the skewer test that comes out clean from the deepest part of the cake.

8. When cake has baked, let it cool in the pan for 10 minutes, then take it out by turning the pan on a wire rack and cool it for 30 minutes.

9.   Meanwhile, prepare the glaze and for this, place all its ingredients in a small bowl and whisk until well combined.

10. Once the cake has cooled, drizzle glaze on it, cut it into eight slices and then serve.

Apple Bundt Cake

Preparation time: 15 minutes

Cooking time: 80 minutes

Total time: 95 minutes

Servings: 12

Nutritional Info (Per Serving):

550 kCal | 29.8 g Fat | 9 g Protein | 68 g Carbs | 4.9 g Fiber | 40 g Sugar

Ingredients:

For the Cake:

1 ¼ cups / 300 ml canola oil

2 cups / 400-grams granulated white sugar, packed

3 large eggs, at room temperature

3 cups / 375-grams flour

½ teaspoon salt

1 ¼ teaspoons baking soda

2 teaspoons vanilla extract, unsweetened

3 cups / 455-grams chopped apples

1 cup chopped pecans

For the Icing:

4 tablespoons caramel dessert topping

1 teaspoon vanilla extract, unsweetened

2 cups / 240-grams powdered sugar

2 tablespoons unsalted butter, softened, and more for greasing

6 tablespoons milk, unsweetened

Directions:

1.   Switch on the oven, set it to 325 °F / 165 °C, and let it preheat.

2.   Meanwhile, take a large bowl, crack eggs in it, and then beat in oil and sugar until combined.

3.   Take a medium bowl, add flour in it, stir in baking soda and salt, and then whisk into the egg mixture, 3 tablespoons at a time, until incorporated.

4.   Stir in vanilla until combined, and then fold in apples and pecans.

5.   Take a 12 cup /3-liter Bundt pan, grease it with melted butter, dust it with flour, then add prepared cake batter in it and bake for 70 to 80 minutes until thoroughly cooked and pass the skewer test that comes out clean from the deepest part of the cake.

6.   When cake has baked, let it cool in the pan for 10 minutes, then take it out by turning the pan on a wire rack and cool it for 30 minutes.

7.   Meanwhile, prepare the icing and for this, place all its ingredients in a medium bowl and beat until well combined, set aside until required

8.   Once the cake has cooled, drizzle icing on it, cut it into twelve slices, and then serve.

Apple and Honey Cake

Preparation time: 15 minutes

Cooking time: 55 minutes

Total time: 70 minutes

Servings: 12

Nutritional Info (Per Serving):

461 kCal | 23.6 g Fat | 5.2 g Protein | 59.4 g Carbs | 2.3 g Fiber |
37.3 g Sugar

Ingredients:

3 medium apples, peeled, cored, shredded

2 ½ cups / 310-grams white all-purpose flour, sifted, leveled

1 cup / 200-grams granulated white sugar, packed

1 teaspoon cinnamon

1 teaspoon baking powder

¼ teaspoon ground allspice

1 teaspoon salt

1 teaspoon baking soda

¾ cup / 90-grams chopped walnuts

¾ cup / 250-grams honey

1 cup / 220 ml olive oil

1 teaspoon vanilla extract, unsweetened

2 large eggs, at room temperature

Directions:

1.   Switch on the oven, set it to 325 °F / 165 °Cand let it preheat.

2.   Meanwhile, take a large bowl, add oil in it, stir in sugar, beat in eggs, one at a time, until fluffy, and then whisk in vanilla and honey until combined.

3. Take a medium bowl, add flour in it, stir in salt, baking soda, allspice, cinnamon, and baking powder and stir until mixed.

4. Stir the flour mixture into the egg mixture and then fold in apples and walnuts until combined.

5. Take a 12 cup / 3-liter Bundt pan, grease it with melted butter, dust it with flour, then add prepared cake batter in it and bake for 50 - 55 minutes until thoroughly cooked and pass the skewer test that comes out clean from the deepest part of the cake.

6. When cake has baked, let it cool in the pan for 10 minutes, then take it out by turning the pan on a wire rack and cool it for 30 minutes.

7. Once the cake has cooled, cut it into twelve slices, and then serve.

Blueberry Bundt Cake

Preparation time: 15 minutes

Cooking time: 60 minutes

Total time: 75 minutes

Servings: 12

Nutritional Info (Per Serving):

490 kCal | 22.5 g Fat | 6.2 g Protein | 66.9 g Carbs | 2.7 g Fiber |
16.3 g Sugar

Ingredients:

For the Cake:

2 cups / 400-grams fresh blueberries

3 cups / 375-grams white all-purpose flour, sifted, leveled

1 teaspoon salt

3 teaspoons baking powder

1 ⅔ cup / 335-grams granulated white sugar, packed

1 teaspoon baking soda

2 teaspoons vanilla extract, unsweetened

¾ cup / 170-grams unsalted butter, softened, and more for greasing

4 large eggs, at room temperature

1 cup / 235-grams sour cream

For the Icing:

1/8 teaspoon salt

1 ½ cups / 180-grams powdered sugar

½ teaspoon vanilla extract, unsweetened

1 tablespoon unsalted butter, softened

3 tablespoons milk, unsweetened

Directions:

1.   Switch on the oven, then set it to 350 °F / 175 °C, and let it preheat.

2.   Meanwhile, take a medium bowl, add flour in it, stir in salt, baking powder, and soda, and set aside until required.

3.   Take a large bowl, add butter in it, beat in sugar until fluffy and then beat in eggs, one at a time, until blended.

4.   Beat in vanilla, and flour mixture and sour cream alternately until well blended and then fold in berries.

5.   Take a 12 cup / 3-liter Bundt pan, grease it with melted butter, dust it with flour, then add prepared cake batter in it and bake for 50 to 60 minutes until thoroughly cooked and pass the skewer test that comes out clean from the deepest part of the cake.

6.   When cake has baked, let it cool in the pan for 10 minutes, then take it out by turning the pan on a wire rack and cool it for 30 minutes.

7.   Meanwhile, prepare the icing and for this, place all its ingredients in a bowl and stir until well combined, set aside until required

8.   Once the cake has cooled, drizzle icing on it, cut it into twelve slices, and then serve.

Chocolate Bundt Cake

Preparation time: 15 minutes

Cooking time: 50 minutes

Total time: 65 minutes

Servings: 12

Nutritional Info (Per Serving):

458 kCal | 21.4 g Fat | 7.4 g Protein | 61.6 g Carbs | 3.2 g Fiber |
8.3 g Sugar

Ingredients:

2 cups / 250-grams white all-purpose flour, sifted, leveled

2 cups / 400-grams granulated white sugar, packed

½ teaspoon salt

1 teaspoon baking soda

1 cup / 200-grams cocoa, unsweetened

1 tablespoon vanilla extract, unsweetened

2 large egg whites, at room temperature

½ cup / 115-grams unsalted butter, softened, and more for greasing

3 large eggs, at room temperature

⅔ cup / 160 ml milk, unsweetened

⅓ cup / 80 ml strong coffee, chilled

Directions:

1.   Switch on the oven, set it to 350 °F / 175 °C, and let it preheat.

2.   Meanwhile, take a medium bowl, add flour in it and stir in baking soda, cocoa, and salt until well mixed.

3.   Take a large bowl, add butter in it, beat in sugar until fluffy, beat in eggs and egg whites, one at a time, and then beat in vanilla until smooth.

4.   Take a small bowl, pour in coffee, add milk, and stir until combined.

5.   Beat in one-third of the flour mixture into the egg mixture, beat in half of the coffee mixture, and then beat in another one-third of the flour mixture.

6.   Beat in the coffee mixture and then beat in the remaining flour mixture until incorporated and smooth.

7.   Take a 12 cup / 3-liter Bundt pan, grease it with melted butter, dust it with flour, then add prepared cake batter in it and bake for 40 to 50 minutes until thoroughly cooked and pass the skewer test that comes out clean from the deepest part of the cake.

8.   When cake has baked, let it cool in the pan for 10 minutes, then take it out by turning the pan on a wire rack and cool it for 30 minutes.

9.   Once the cake has cooled, cut it into twelve slices, and then serve.

Cinnamon Swirl Coffee Bundt Cake

Preparation time: 15 minutes

Cooking time: 48 minutes

Total time: 63 minutes

Servings: 12

Nutritional Info (Per Serving):

405 kCal | 41.3 g Fat | 2.8 g Protein | 49.4 g Carbs | 1 g Fiber | 24 g Sugar

Ingredients:

2 ½ cups / 315-grams white all-purpose flour, sifted, leveled

½ cup / 60-grams chopped walnuts

1 teaspoon baking powder

1 ¾ cups / 350-grams granulated white sugar, packed, divided

1 teaspoon baking soda

1 tablespoon ground cinnamon

1 teaspoon vanilla extract, unsweetened

¾ cup / 170-grams unsalted butter, softened, and more for greasing

3 large eggs, at room temperature

1 cup / 235-grams sour cream

Directions:

1.   Switch on the oven, set it to 400 °F / 200 °C and let it preheat.

2.   Meanwhile, take a large bowl, add butter in it, beat in 1 ½ cups / 290 grams sugar until combined, then beat in eggs, one at a time, and beat in vanilla until blended.

3.   Take a medium bowl, add flour in it, stir baking powder and soda, then gradually flour mixture and sour cream alternately until well blended and fold in walnuts until mixed.

4.   Take a 10 cup / 2.5-liter Bundt pan, grease it with melted butter, dust it with flour, and then add half of the prepared cake batter in it.

5.   Stir together remaining sugar and cinnamon, sprinkle this mixture over cake batter in the pan, and cover with remaining cake batter.

6.   Bake for 8 minutes, switch heat to 350 °F / 175 °C, and continue baking for 40 minutes until thoroughly cooked and pass the skewer test that comes out clean from the deepest part of the cake.

7.   When cake has baked, let it cool in the pan for 10 minutes, then take it out by turning the pan on a wire rack and cool it for 30 minutes.

8.   Once the cake has cooled, cut it into twelve slices, and then serve.

Sour Cream and Lemon Cake

Preparation time: 15 minutes

Cooking time: 55 minutes

Total time: 70 minutes

Servings: 12

Nutritional Info (Per Serving):

306 kCal | 19.2 g Fat | 2.7 g Protein | 33 g Carbs | 1.6 g Fiber | 15g Sugar

Ingredients:

For the Cake:

2 cups / 250-grams white all-purpose flour, sifted, leveled

1 lemon, zested

2 cups / 400-grams granulated white sugar, packed

2 teaspoons baking powder

1 teaspoon salt

1 cup / 235-grams sour cream

1 cup / 230-grams unsalted butter, softened, and more for greasing

3 large eggs, at room temperature

For the Glaze:

2 tablespoons lemon juice

2 cups / 240-grams confectioner's sugar

¼ cup / 60-grams unsalted butter, melted

Directions:

1.   Switch on the oven, set it to 325 °F / 165 °C and let it preheat.

2.   Meanwhile, take a medium bowl, add flour in it, stir in salt and baking powder, and set aside until required.

3.   Take a large bowl, add butter in it and beat in sugar until fluffy.

4.   Then beat in eggs, one at a time, beat in lemon zest until combined, and then gradually beat in flour mixture and sour cream alternately until incorporated.

5.   Take a 12 cup / 3-liter Bundt pan, grease it with melted butter, dust it with flour, then add prepared cake batter in it and bake for 55 minutes until thoroughly cooked and pass the skewer test that comes out clean from the deepest part of the cake.

6.   When cake has baked, let it cool in the pan for 10 minutes, then take it out by turning the pan on a wire rack and cool it for 30 minutes.

7.   Meanwhile, prepare the glaze and for this, place all its ingredients in a small bowl and whisk until blended, set aside until required.

8.   Once the cake has cooled, drizzle glaze on it, cut it into twelve slices and then serve.

Brown Sugar Bundt Cake with Caramel Glaze

Preparation time: 15 minutes

Cooking time: 65 minutes

Total time: 80 minutes

Servings: 14

Nutritional Info (Per Serving):

422 kCal | 15.9 g Fat | 4.7 g Protein | 69 g Carbs | 12.3 g Fiber | 49 g Sugar

Ingredients:

For the Cake:

3 cups / 375-grams white all-purpose flour, sifted, leveled

½ cup / 100-grams granulated white sugar, packed

2½ cups / 490-grams brown sugar, packed

½ teaspoon baking soda

1 teaspoon salt

1 tablespoon vanilla extract, unsweetened

1 cup / 230-grams unsalted butter, softened, and more for greasing

1 cup /245 ml buttermilk

5 large eggs, at room temperature

For the Glaze:

1 cup / 195-grams brown sugar

2 teaspoons vanilla extract, unsweetened

¾ cup / 170-grams unsalted butter, softened

½ cup / 120 ml milk, unsweetened

Directions:

1.   Switch on the oven, set it to 350 °F / 175 °C, and let it preheat.

2.   Meanwhile, take a medium bowl, add flour in it, add salt and baking soda and stir until mixed, set aside until required.

3.   Take a large bowl, add butter in it, beat in white and brown sugar until fluffy, beat in vanilla until combined, and then beat in flour and buttermilk alternately until incorporated.

4.   Take a 12 cup / 3-liter Bundt pan, grease it with melted butter, dust it with flour, then add prepared cake batter in it and bake for 55 to 65 minutes until thoroughly cooked and pass the skewer test that comes out clean from the deepest part of the cake.

5.   When cake has baked, let it cool in the pan for 10 minutes, then take it out by turning the pan on a wire rack and cool it for 30 minutes.

6.   Meanwhile, prepare the glaze and for this, take a medium saucepan, add butter and sugar in it, pour in milk, stir and bring the mixture to boil.

7.   Switch heat to medium-low heat, simmer the glaze for 2 minutes, then remove the pan from heat, stir in vanilla, and set aside until required.

8.   Once the cake has cooled, drizzle glaze on it, cut it into fourteen slices and then serve.

Ricotta Cake with Browned Butter Glaze

Preparation time: 15 minutes

Cooking time: 90 minutes

Total time: 105 minutes

Servings: 12

Nutritional Info (Per Serving):

465 kCal | 21.8 g Fat | 6.7 g Protein | 61 g Carbs | 2.1 g Fiber | 8.2 g Sugar

Ingredients:

For the Cake:

3 cups / 375-grams all-purpose flour

1 ½ cups / 290-grams brown sugar, packed

¼ teaspoon salt

1 cup / 200-grams granulated white sugar, packed

¼ teaspoon baking soda

1 tablespoon vanilla extract, unsweetened

1 cup / 230-grams unsalted butter, softened, and more for greasing

1 cup / 125-grams ricotta cheese

6 large eggs, at room temperature, separated

For the Glaze:

1 ¾ cups / 210-grams powdered sugar

2 teaspoons vanilla extract unsweetened

1/3 cup / 75-grams unsalted butter, softened

1/3 / 70 ml milk

Directions:

1.   Switch on the oven, set it to 350 °F / 175 °C, and let it preheat.

2.   Meanwhile, take a medium bowl, add flour in it along with salt and baking soda and stir until mixed.

3.   Take a large bowl, place butter, beat in cheese, beat in both sugars until fluffy, and then beat in yolks, one at a time, until blended.

4.   Beat in vanilla and then gradually beat in flour mixture until incorporated.

5.   Take another large bowl, place egg whites in it, beat until stiff peaks come together, and then fold into the batter until mixed.

6.   Take a 12 cup / 3-liter Bundt pan, grease it with melted butter, dust it with flour, then add prepared cake batter in it and bake for 75 to 90 minutes until thoroughly cooked and pass the skewer test that comes out clean from the deepest part of the cake.

7.   When cake has baked, let it cool in the pan for 10 minutes, then take it out by turning the pan on a wire rack and cool it for 30 minutes.

8.   Meanwhile, prepare the glaze and for this, take a small saucepan, place it over medium heat, add butter and cook for 10 minutes until golden, stirring constantly.

9. Remove pan from heat, pour the butter into a medium bowl, add milk and sugar and stir until smooth, set aside until required.

10. Once the cake has cooled, drizzle glaze on it, cut it into twelve slices and then serve.

Chocolate and Raspberry Bundt Cake

Preparation time: 15 minutes

Cooking time: 60 minutes

Total time: 75 minutes

Servings: 12

Nutritional Info (Per Serving):

340 kCal | 18 g Fat | 3.5 g Protein | 44 g Carbs | 3.9 g Fiber | 36 g Sugar

Ingredients:

For the Cake:

1 ⅓ cup / 170-grams fresh raspberries

2 ½ cups / 315-grams white all-purpose flour, sifted, leveled

1 orange, zested

½ teaspoon salt

2 teaspoons baking powder

1½ cups / 300-grams granulated white sugar, packed

1 cup / 180-grams chocolate chips, semi-sweet

1 teaspoon vanilla extract, unsweetened

½ teaspoon orange extract, unsweetened

1 cup / 230-grams butter, softened, and more for greasing

3 large eggs, at room temperature

1 ⅓ cups / 315 ml buttermilk

For the Glaze:

2 tablespoons raspberry jelly

1 ⅓ cup / 170-grams fresh raspberries

½ cup / 90-grams chocolate chips, semi-sweet

2 tablespoons milk, unsweetened

Directions:

1.   Switch on the oven, set it to 350 °F / 175 °C, and let it preheat.

2.   Meanwhile, take a medium bowl, add flour in it along with salt and baking powder, stir until mixed, and set aside until required.

3.   Take a large bowl, add butter in it, beat in sugar until fluffy, and then beat in orange zest, vanilla, and orange extracts.

4.   Beat in eggs, one at a time, until combined and then beat in flour and buttermilk alternately until incorporated and then fold in berries and chocolate chips until mixed.

5.   Take an 8 cup / 2-liter Bundt pan, grease it with melted butter, dust it with flour, then add prepared cake batter in it and bake for 50 to 60 minutes until thoroughly cooked and pass the skewer test that comes out clean from the deepest part of the cake.

6.   When cake has baked, let it cool in the pan for 10 minutes, then take it out by turning the pan on a wire rack and cool it for 30 minutes.

7.   Meanwhile, prepare the glaze and for this, take a medium heatproof bowl, add raspberry jelly, chocolate chips and milk and microwave for 30 seconds until chocolate has melted, set aside until required.

8.   Once the cake has cooled, drizzle glaze on it, cut it into twelve slices, and then serve with fresh raspberries.

Raspberry and Blueberry Bundt Cake

Preparation time: 15 minutes

Cooking time: 65 minutes

Total time: 80 minutes

Servings: 12

Nutritional Info (Per Serving):

467 kCal | 20.1 g Fat | 7 g Protein | 65.3 g Carbs | 3.2 g Fiber | 19.5 g Sugar

Ingredients:

For the Cake:

1 cup / 100-grams fresh blueberries

3 cups / 375-grams white all-purpose flour, sifted, leveled

1 cup / 125-grams frozen raspberries

1 ½ cups / 300-grams granulated white sugar, packed

3 teaspoons baking powder

½ teaspoon salt

1 teaspoon baking soda

2 teaspoons vanilla extract, unsweetened

¾ cup / 170-grams unsalted butter, softened, and more for greasing

4 large eggs, at room temperature

¾ cup / 180 ml buttermilk

For the Glaze:

1 ½ cups / 180-grams powdered sugar

½ teaspoon vanilla extract, unsweetened

3 tablespoons unsalted butter, softened

2 tablespoons hot water, or more as needed

Directions:

1.   Switch on the oven, set it to 350 °F / 175 °C, and let it preheat.

2.   Meanwhile, take a medium bowl, add flour in it, reserving 2 tablespoons of flour, add salt, baking powder and soda and stir until mixed.

3.   Take a large bowl, add butter, beat in sugar until fluffy, and then beat in eggs, one at a time, until blended.

10.   Beat in vanilla, beat in one-third of the flour mixture into the egg mixture, beat in half of the buttermilk, and then beat in another one-third of the flour mixture.

4.   Beat in remaining buttermilk and then beat in remaining flour mixture until incorporated and smooth.

5.   Take a medium bowl, add both berries in it, sprinkle with reserved flour, toss until well coated, and then fold berries into the prepared batter.

6.   Take a 10 cup / 2.5-liter Bundt pan, grease it with melted butter, dust it with flour, then add prepared cake batter in it and bake for 55 to 65 minutes until thoroughly cooked and pass the skewer test that comes out clean from the deepest part of the cake.

7.   When cake has baked, let it cool in the pan for 10 minutes, then take it out by turning the pan on a wire rack and cool it for 30 minutes.

8.   Meanwhile, prepare the glaze and for this, place all its ingredients in a medium bowl, and beat well until glaze reaches to desired consistency, set aside until required.

9.   Once the cake has cooled, drizzle glaze sugar on it, cut it into twelve slices and then serve.

Cream Cheese Bundt Cake

Preparation time: 15 minutes

Cooking time: 80 minutes

Total time: 95 minutes

Servings: 14

Nutritional Info (Per Serving):

530 kCal | 29 g Fat | 6.2 g Protein | 67 g Carbs | 1 g Fiber | 43.7 g Sugar

Ingredients:

3 cups / 375-grams white all-purpose flour, sifted, leveled

3 cups / 600-grams granulated white sugar, packed

1 teaspoon vanilla extract, unsweetened

1 ½ cups / 340-grams unsalted butter, softened

1 cup / 225-grams cream cheese, softened

6 large eggs, at room temperature

Directions:

1. Switch on the oven, set it to 325 °F / 165 °C and let it preheat.

2. Meanwhile, take a large bowl, add butter in it, whisk in cream cheese until smooth and then gradually beat in sugar until fluffy.

3. Then beat in eggs, one at a time, gradually beat in flour until incorporated and beat in vanilla until combined.

4. Take a 12 cup / 3-liter Bundt pan, grease it with melted butter, dust it with flour, then add prepared cake batter in it and bake for 80 minutes until thoroughly cooked and pass the skewer test that comes out clean from the deepest part of the cake.

5.   When cake has baked, let it cool in the pan for 10 minutes, then take it out by turning the pan on a wire rack and cool it for 30 minutes.

6.   Once the cake has cooled, cut it into fourteen slices, and then serve.

Fruity Bundt Cake

Preparation time: 15 minutes

Cooking time: 90 minutes

Total time: 105 minutes

Servings: 12

Nutritional Info (Per Serving):

620 kCal | 36.5 g Fat | 5.8 g Protein | 71.2 g Carbs | 3.6 g Fiber | 43 g Sugar

Ingredients:

1 cup / 225-grams crushed pineapple

1 cup / 100-grams fresh blueberries

2 bananas, peeled, diced

3 cups / 375-grams white all-purpose flour, sifted, leveled

½ teaspoon cinnamon

1 teaspoon salt

½ teaspoon ground nutmeg

2 cups / 400-grams granulated white sugar, packed

½ cup / 40-grams flaked coconut

1 cup/ 120-grams chopped pecans

1 teaspoon baking soda

3 teaspoons vanilla extract, unsweetened

1 ½ cups / 355 ml olive oil

3 large eggs, at room temperature

Directions:

1.   Switch on the oven, set it to 350 °F / 175 °C, and let it preheat.

2.   Meanwhile, take a medium bowl, add flour in it, add nutmeg, baking soda, salt, and cinnamon, stir and set aside until required.

3.   Take a large bowl, crack eggs in it and beat in sugar, vanilla, and oil until smooth, then gradually whisk in flour until incorporated and stir in banana, pineapple, berries, and pecans until mixed.

4.   Take a 12 cup / 3-liter Bundt pan, grease it with melted butter, dust it with flour, then add prepared cake batter in it and bake for 75 to 90 minutes until thoroughly cooked and pass the skewer test that comes out clean from the deepest part of the cake.

5.   When cake has baked, let it cool in the pan for 10 minutes, then take it out by turning the pan on a wire rack and cool it for 30 minutes.

6.   Once the cake has cooled, cut it into twelve slices, and then serve.

Lemon Coconut Cake

Preparation time: 15 minutes

Cooking time: 60 minutes

Total time: 75 minutes

Servings: 12

Nutritional Info (Per Serving):

417 kCal | 20 g Fat | 4.2 g Protein | 59.5 g Carbs | 1.2 g Fiber | 34.1g Sugar

Ingredients:

For the Cake:

3 cups / 375-grams white all-purpose flour, sifted, leveled

1 ½ cups / 115-grams shredded coconut

2 teaspoons baking powder

1 teaspoon salt

1 teaspoon baking soda

3 tablespoon lemon zest

1 ½ cups / 300-grams granulated white sugar, packed

½ cup / 120 ml lemon juice

2 teaspoons vanilla extract, unsweetened

⅔ cups / 155 ml olive oil

1 ⅔ cup / 400 ml coconut milk, unsweetened

For the Icing:

2 tablespoons lemon juice

1 cup / 120-grams powdered sugar

Directions:

1.   Switch on the oven, set it to 350 °F / 175 °C, and let it preheat.

2.   Meanwhile, take a large bowl, add oil and milk in it and beat in vanilla and lemon juice and zest.

3.   Gradually beat in flour, baking powder, and soda until incorporated and then whisk in coconut and salt until combined.

4.   Take a 12 cup / 3-liter Bundt pan, grease it with oil, dust it with flour, then add prepared cake batter in it and bake for 1 hour until thoroughly cooked and pass the skewer test that comes out clean from the deepest part of the cake.

5.   When cake has baked, let it cool in the pan for 10 minutes, then take it out by turning the pan on a wire rack and cool it for 30 minutes.

6.   Meanwhile, prepare the icing and for this, place all its ingredients in a small bowl and whisk until mixed, set aside until required.

7.   Once the cake has cooled, drizzle icing sugar on it, cut it into twelve slices and then serve.

Lemon Yogurt Bundt Cake

Preparation time: 15 minutes

Cooking time: 60 minutes

Total time: 75 minutes

Servings: 16

Nutritional Info (Per Serving):

320 kCal | 17 g Fat | 3.2 g Protein | 45.3 g Carbs | 1.1 g Fiber |
22.3 g Sugar

Ingredients:

For the Cake:

3 cups / 375-grams white all-purpose flour, sifted, leveled

2 teaspoons baking powder

3 tablespoons cornstarch

1 teaspoon baking soda

½ teaspoon salt

½ cup / 120 ml lemon juice

2 lemons, zested

1 cup / 200-grams granulated white sugar, packed

2 teaspoons vanilla extract, unsweetened

1 cup / 220 ml olive oil

2 cups / 490-grams cashew yogurt

For the Lemon Syrup:

¼ cup / 60 ml lemon juice

¼ cup /50-grams granulated white sugar, packed

For the Lemon Glaze:

1/3 cup / 80 ml lemon juice

¾ cup / 90-grams powdered sugar

Directions:

1.   Switch on the oven, set it to 350 °F / 175 °C, and let it preheat.

2.   Meanwhile, take a medium bowl, add flour in it and stir in salt, cornstarch, baking powder, and soda, set aside until required.

3. Take a large bowl, add cashew yogurt in it, beat in sugar, oil, vanilla, lemon zest, and juice until combined, and then gradually beat in flour mixture in four batches until incorporated.

4.   Take a 12 cup / 3-liter Bundt pan, grease it with oil, dust it with flour, then add prepared cake batter in it and bake for 50 to 60 minutes until thoroughly cooked and pass the skewer test that comes out clean from the deepest part of the cake.

5.   Meanwhile, prepare the syrup and for this, place a small saucepan over medium heat, add sugar, cook it for 5 minutes until it has melted, and then stir in lemon juice, set aside until required.

6. When cake has baked, poke holes in it, drizzle with prepared syrup and let the cake rest in the pan for 10 minutes until all the sauce has absorbed.

7. Then take out the cake by turning the pan on a plate and cool it for 30 minutes.

8.   Meanwhile, prepare the glaze and for this, place its ingredients in a small bowl and whisk until well combined.

9.   Once the cake has cooled, drizzle glaze on it, cut it into sixteen slices and then serve.

Gingerbread Bundt Cake

Preparation time: 15 minutes

Cooking time: 50 minutes

Total time: 65 minutes

Servings: 12

Nutritional Info (Per Serving):

391 kCal | 17.6 g Fat | 6.2 g Protein | 60.2 g Carbs | 5.5 g Fiber |
30 g Sugar

Ingredients:

3 cups / 375-grams white all-purpose flour, sifted, leveled

3 teaspoons baking powder

½ teaspoon nutmeg

½ teaspoon salt

½ teaspoon cloves

1 cup / 195-grams brown sugar, packed

2 ½ teaspoons ground ginger

¾ cup / 150-grams molasses

1 teaspoon cinnamon

3 teaspoons baking soda

½ teaspoon vanilla extract, unsweetened

¾ cup / 155-grams coconut oil

1 ½ cups / 355 ml almond milk, unsweetened

¾ cup / 190-grams applesauce, unsweetened

Directions:

1.   Switch on the oven, set it to 350 °F / 175 °C, and let it preheat.

2.   Meanwhile, take a medium bowl, place flour in it, and then stir in cinnamon, cloves, nutmeg, ginger, salt, baking soda, and powder until combined.

3.   Take a large bowl, add oil in it, beat in sugar until fluffy, beat in molasses, milk, and apple sauce until well combined and then beat in flour mixture in four batches until incorporated.

4.   Take a 12 cup / 3-liter Bundt pan, grease it with melted butter, dust it with flour, then add prepared cake batter in it and bake for 40 to 50 minutes until thoroughly cooked and pass the skewer test that comes out clean from the deepest part of the cake.

5.   When cake has baked, let it cool in the pan for 10 minutes, then take it out by turning the pan on a wire rack and cool it for 30 minutes.

6.   Once the cake has cooled, cut it into twelve slices, and then serve.

Chocolate Pumpkin Cake

Preparation time: 15 minutes

Cooking time: 70 minutes

Total time: 85 minutes

Servings: 12

Nutritional Info (Per Serving):

265 kCal | 10.2 g Fat | 3.1 g Protein | 48.4 g Carbs | 2.5 g Fiber | 28 g Sugar

Ingredients:

1 ¾ cups / 220-grams white all-purpose flour, sifted, leveled

1 ½ teaspoon baking soda

½ teaspoon ground ginger

2 cups / 400-grams granulated white sugar, packed

¾ tablespoon salt

1 ½ teaspoon baking powder

¼ teaspoon ground nutmeg

1 teaspoon cinnamon

¾ cup / 85-grams cocoa powder, unsweetened

1/3 cup / 65-grams maple syrup

1 tablespoon lemon juice

2 teaspoon vanilla extract, unsweetened

½ cup / 120 ml canola oil

1 cup / 235 ml soy milk

1 ¾ cup / 395-grams pumpkin puree

½ cup / 100-grams vegan ganache, for icing

Directions:

1. Switch on the oven, set it to 350 °F / 175 °C, and let it preheat.

2. Meanwhile, take a small bowl, pour in milk, stir in lemon juice, and let it sit for 5 minutes until thickened, set aside until required.

3. Take a medium bowl, add flour in it, add ginger, salt, nutmeg, cinnamon, cocoa powder, baking powder, and soda and stir until mixed.

4. Take a large bowl, add oil in it and beat in vanilla, sugar, oil, and maple syrup until smooth.

5. Beat in pumpkin puree until smooth and then beat in flour mixture and milk mixture alternately in four batches until incorporated.

6. Take a 12 cup / 3-liter Bundt pan, grease it with oil, dust it with flour, then add prepared cake batter in it and bake for 60 to 70 minutes until thoroughly cooked and pass the skewer test that comes out clean from the deepest part of the cake.

7. When cake has baked, let it cool in the pan for 10 minutes, then take it out by turning the pan on a wire rack and cool it for 30 minutes.

8. Once the cake has cooled, drizzle vegan ganache on it, cut it into twelve slices and then serve.

Eggless Chocolate Bundt Cake

Preparation time: 15 minutes

Cooking time: 50 minutes

Total time: 65 minutes

Servings: 12

Nutritional Info (Per Serving):

270 kCal | 13 g Fat | 3.7 g Protein | 41 g Carbs | 1.4 g Fiber |
24.2g Sugar

Ingredients:

2 ¼ cups / 280-grams white all-purpose flour, sifted, leveled

½ teaspoon salt

¾ cup / 150-grams granulated white sugar, packed

½ cup / 55-grams cocoa powder

½ cup / 100-grams brown sugar, packed

1 teaspoon baking soda

1 teaspoon vanilla extract, unsweetened

0.56 cup / 130 ml olive oil, and more for greasing

1 tablespoon apple cider vinegar

1 cup / 235 ml water

Directions:

1.   Switch on the oven, then it to 350 °F / 175 °C, and let it preheat.

2.   Meanwhile, take a large bowl, add flour in it and stir in cocoa until mixed.

3.   Whisk in both sugars, salt, and baking soda until combined, then pour in oil, vinegar, vanilla, and water and continue whisking until smooth batter comes together.

4.   Take a 12 cup / 3-liter Bundt pan, grease it with oil, dust it with flour, then add prepared cake batter in it and bake for 45 to

50 minutes until thoroughly cooked and pass the skewer test that comes out clean from the deepest part of the cake.

5.   When cake has baked, let it cool in the pan for 10 minutes, then take it out by turning the pan on a wire rack and cool it for 30 minutes.

6.   Once the cake has cooled, cut it into twelve slices, and then serve.

Banana Bundt Cake

Preparation time: 15 minutes

Cooking time: 50 minutes

Total time: 65 minutes

Servings: 12

Nutritional Info (Per Serving):

190 kCal | 5.2 g Fat | 4.1 g Protein | 40.1 g Carbs | 2.2 g Fiber | 20.1 g Sugar

Ingredients:

For the Cake:

½ cup / 100-grams mashed banana

1 ⅓ cup / 165-grams white all-purpose flour, sifted, leveled

¼ cup / 55-grams cane sugar

1 teaspoon baking powder

¼ cup / 50-grams agave syrup

½ teaspoon salt

½ teaspoon baking soda

2 tablespoons coconut oil, melted, and more for greasing

1 teaspoon vanilla extract, unsweetened

2 tablespoons apple cider vinegar

½ cup / 115-grams coconut milk, unsweetened

For the Glaze:

1 ½ cup / 180-grams powdered sugar

¾ tablespoon lemon juice

Directions:

1.   Switch on the oven, set it to 350 °F / 175 °C, and let it preheat.

2.   Meanwhile, take a medium bowl, add flour in it, add salt, cane sugar, baking powder, and soda and stir until mixed.

3.   Take a large bowl, add mashed banana in it, beat in vanilla, oil, lemon juice, agave, and milk until blended and then blend in flour mixture in four batches until incorporated.

4.   Take a 6 cup / 1.5-liter Bundt pan, grease it with oil, dust it with flour, then add prepared cake batter in it and bake for 40 to 50 minutes until thoroughly cooked and pass the skewer test that comes out clean from the deepest part of the cake.

5.   When cake has baked, let it cool in the pan for 10 minutes, then take it out by turning the pan on a wire rack and cool it for 30 minutes.

6.   Meanwhile, prepare the glaze and for this, place all its ingredients in a small bowl and whisk well until combined.

7.   Once the cake has cooled, drizzle glaze on it, cut it into twelve slices and then serve.

Thanks for buying *Bundt Cake Recipes!*

If you found the recipes amazing and delicious, please leave a 5-star review on Amazon to support the author's work.

About The Author

Marie Folher grew up in Strasbourg, France and she fell in love with baking as a kid. She moved to California at the age of 21 and she found a job from a small bakery. Since then, she has baked countless amount of different baked goods. She has had time to experiment many different flavour combinations, and with trial and error she has found, and still finds, amazing recipes. With her cookbooks, she wants to share her best recipes with you.

Books by Marie Folher

Bundt Cake Recipes – 30
Delicious Bundt Cake Recipes
From Scratch

Keto Chaffle Recipes – 30
Easy Fast and Super Delicious
Ketogenic Chaffle Recipes

Keto Bread Machine Recipes
– 30 Easy, Healthy and Low-
Carb Ketogenic Bread
Machine Recipes

Keto Bread Recipes – 30
Easy, Healthy and Super
Delicious Low-Carb
Ketogenic Bread Recipes

Artisan Bread Recipes –
Artisan Bread Cookbook Full
of Easy, Simple And
Mouthwatering Artisan Bread
Recipes

Bread Machine Cookbook –
Simple and Easy-To-Follow
Bread Machine Recipes for
Mouthwatering Homemade
Bread

Image Credits

Marbled Bundt Cake with Almond and Chocolate: iStock.com/Fudio

Banana and Chocolate Bundt Cake: iStock.com/ALLEKO

Blood Orange and Olive Oil Bundt Cake: iStock.com/Lara Hata

Banana Date Cake: iStock.com/AnastasiaNurullina

Soured Cream Bundt Cake: iStock.com/manyakotic

Chocolate Peppermint Bundt Cake: iStock.com/bhofack2

Monkey Bread: iStock.com/Galiyah Assan

Grapefruit and Poppy Seed Cake: iStock.com/QuietJosephine

Lemon Poppy Seed Bundt Cake: iStock.com/Ivannag82

Blood Orange Cake: iStock.com/StephanieFrey

Butter Bundt Cake: iStock.com/jirkaejc

Lemon Lavender Cake: iStock.com/seregalsv

Apple Bundt Cake: iStock.com/KateSmirnova

Apple and Honey Cake: iStock.com/Studio Doros

Blueberry Bundt Cake: iStock.com/IriGri8

Chocolate Bundt Cake: iStock.com/YelenaYemchuk

Cinnamon Swirl Coffee Bundt Cake: iStock.com/gavran333

Sour Cream and Lemon Cake: iStock.com/Mariha-kitchen

Brown Sugar Bundt Cake with Caramel Glaze:
iStock.com/rolbos

Ricotta Cake with Browned Butter Glaze: iStock.com/ehaurylik

Chocolate and Raspberry Bundt Cake: iStock.com/jessicaphoto

Raspberry and Blueberry Bundt Cake:
iStock.com/simonidadjordjevic

Cream Cheese Bundt Cake: iStock.com/amberleeknight

Fruity Bundt Cake: iStock.com/5second

Lemon Coconut Cake: iStock.com/bauhaus1000

Lemon Yogurt Bundt Cake: iStock.com/ASIFE

Gingerbread Bundt Cake: iStock.com/Spaziocolore

Chocolate Pumpkin Cake: iStock.com/viennetta

Eggless Chocolate Bundt Cake: iStock.com/bhofack2

Banana Bundt Cake: iStock.com/cmspic

Made in the USA
Middletown, DE
21 June 2021

42872456R00066